The Big

Contents

Nothing at all   2
Starting with a BANG   4
Hotter than the Sun   6
The first "stuff"   8
A bright fog   10
The fog clears   12
The dark age   14
Early stars   16
Spreading stardust   18
The Universe today   20
The Solar System   22
A spiral of stars   28
Groups and clusters   30
Discovering the Big Bang   32
New galaxies   34
The Big Bang theory   36
How do we know?   38
Better telescopes   40
Telescopes in space   42
Seeing in different ways   44
Future discoveries   46
The future Universe   48
Some answers and new questions   50
Glossary   52
Index   53
Big Bang timeline   54

Written by Andrew Solway

Collins

Nothing at all

The Big Bang is the way scientists think the Universe began. It happened deep in the past – about 14 **billion** years ago. This was billions of years before the Earth was formed – even before the Sun began to shine.

The Big Bang was the beginning of everything. Before then, there was nothing at all, not even empty space. In fact, there wasn't even time, so nothing could happen before the Big Bang.

In this book we're going to find out about the moment scientists think the Universe burst into existence, and how they found out about it.

Fact file

The name "Big Bang" suggests that the Universe was born in a huge explosion. But, in fact, when the Universe began, it was incredibly tiny (although it got bigger very fast). And there was no "bang", or any sound at all, because there was no air to carry sound.

People often show the Big Bang as a huge explosion. But it wasn't quite like that.

Starting with a BANG

What was the Big Bang like? No one really knows. All we can say is that there was a sudden burst of energy as the Universe came into existence.

The Universe was extremely small when it began. It was packed into a space too small to see. However, the power of the Big Bang was enormous – far greater than the most powerful **nuclear explosion**.

The hydrogen bomb: the most powerful explosion on Earth. The Big Bang was 100,000 times more powerful.

When a bomb explodes, bits and pieces shoot out at high speed into the surrounding space. But the Big Bang was different. Things didn't fly through space – space itself expanded. It was a bit like a balloon being blown up very, very fast. When you blow up a balloon, the rubber stretches as the balloon gets bigger.

When the Big Bang happened, space stretched like the rubber skin of a balloon.

Hotter than the Sun

In the first moments after the Big Bang, the Universe expanded very, very fast. In a tiny fraction of a second, the Universe became 100 billion **trillion** trillion times bigger! But then expansion slowed right down.

The Universe was now much bigger than before – and incredibly hot. It was billions and billions of degrees hotter than the heart of the Sun. It was so hot that there was nothing solid, and nothing liquid. It was too hot even for gases to form. The whole Universe was just light, heat, and other kinds of energy.

Fact file

Scientists think that just after the Big Bang, the whole of the Universe was about the size of a grain of sand.

Fact file

Energy is what makes things happen in the Universe. Heat, electricity and light are all common kinds of energy.

electricity

light

heat

The first "stuff"

After the first huge expansion, the Universe carried on expanding, but more slowly. As it expanded, it began to cool down. About a second after the Universe began, it became cool enough for matter to form.

Matter is the "stuff" that everything around us is made of. Everything solid, every drop of liquid, and every puff of gas is matter. *We* are matter, too.

These rocks are solid.

The yellowish cloud coming out of this volcano is a gas.

All matter is made up of very tiny particles, too small to see with most microscopes. And these particles are made of even tinier particles! It is these tiniest particles of matter that started to form in the first second of the Universe.

This water is liquid.

A bright fog

As the Universe continued to cool down, the tiniest particles of matter gradually began to join together into slightly larger bits. This went on for many years.

Even though the Universe had cooled down, it was still hotter than the centre of the Sun. When they are very hot, matter particles have lots of energy and rush around. In the early Universe, particles rushed around so fast that they were constantly bashing into light beams and knocking them off-course. The result was that light got bounced around all over the place. If we'd been there, it would have been impossible to see anything. It would have been like being in a very bright, thick fog.

In thick fog, car headlights do not shine far. In the "foggy" universe, light could not travel far.

The fog clears

About 400,000 years after the Big Bang, things had cooled down quite a bit. The temperature of the whole Universe was 3,000°C, about the same as the wire inside a lightbulb. At this temperature, it was possible for gas to form. This gas was mostly hydrogen.

About 400,000 years after the Big Bang, the whole Universe was the temperature of this lightbulb.

When hydrogen started forming, something amazing happened. Particles were no longer so squashed together, and they were not zooming around so fast. Light could travel without being constantly knocked off-course. So the fog cleared, and the Universe became **transparent**.

Fact file

Hydrogen is the lightest and most common **substance** in the Universe. The Sun is made mostly of hydrogen, and so are other stars. There are also many huge clouds of hydrogen gas in space.

The gas in this gas cloud is hydrogen.

The dark age

A million years after the Big Bang, the whole Universe was still hot, and still growing. It was also *boring*. Everywhere was the same – nothing but gas. There were still no stars or planets, nothing solid or liquid.

This was the "dark age" of the Universe. Although there was hot gas everywhere, the gas wasn't hot enough to glow, which meant there were no stars or galaxies to light up space. Everything was pitch black.

After a few million years of darkness, things at last began to happen. In some places, where there was a tiny bit more gas than elsewhere, gravity began to act. The pull of gravity in these areas began to draw in gas from the surroundings. Slowly, massive clouds of gas gathered.

Fact file

Gravity is a force that attracts objects towards each other. The Sun's gravity attracts the Earth and keeps it circling round and round. Earth's gravity keeps the Moon in **orbit**. Gravity also stops everything on Earth from flying off into space – including us!

This dark cloud of gas and dust blocks the light from the stars beyond it. In the "dark age" the whole Universe was as black as this.

Early stars

Between 100 million and 400 million years after the Big Bang, the dark age ended. Smaller balls of gas began to form within the massive clouds of gas that had gathered. Most of the gas in these clouds was hydrogen.

In time, gravity squeezed these hydrogen balls further. The hydrogen got hotter and hotter. Eventually it got so hot that the centre of each hydrogen ball "caught fire" and began to shine brightly. The first ever stars had formed.

Stars can only shine while they have fuel – gas – to burn. The earliest stars were very large and bright. They used up their fuel quickly. The Sun is expected to shine for a total of 10 billion years, but the early stars shone for only a few million years.

From stars to galaxies

Early stars formed in groups. Groups of stars that were fairly close together moved towards each other, attracted by gravity. All over the Universe, small groups of stars joined up to make huge "star islands" with millions of stars. These were the first galaxies.

The earliest stars were hot, blue stars.

Fact file

Not all stars are the same. They vary in size from super-giants 1,000 times bigger than the Sun to dwarfs which are 100 times smaller. The colour of a star shows how hot it is. Hot stars burn bluish white, while cool stars are redder. Usually bigger stars are hotter than small ones. However, some giant stars are red.

Spreading stardust

A billion years after the Big Bang, the Universe was beginning to look the way it does today. But there was one big difference. Today, there are many different elements in the Universe. Elements are simple substances such as iron, oxygen and carbon. We need oxygen to breathe and iron for our blood, and carbon is the most important element in all living things.

In the early Universe, there was no iron, oxygen, or carbon. There was only hydrogen and small amounts of two other elements. So where did all the other elements in the Universe come from? The answer is, they were cooked up in stars.

Cooking up new substances

Hydrogen is the fuel that makes stars shine. As the hydrogen is used up, it turns into another element called helium. When the hydrogen runs out, the helium becomes the main fuel for the star instead. As the helium is used up it turns into carbon, oxygen and other elements.

Eventually, the star has nothing left to use as fuel. If it is very big, like the early stars, it swells up and bursts in a huge explosion called a supernova.

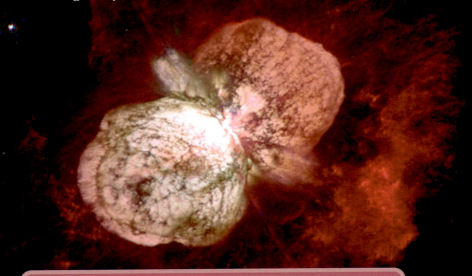

This giant star is surrounded by clouds of dust, which are produced by violent explosions on its surface. The star will eventually explode in a huge supernova.

When the first stars exploded, they scattered "stardust" across the Universe. This stardust contained the new elements that had been cooked up inside them. So, when new stars formed, they contained some of this stardust.

For over 12 billion years, stars have been cooking up new substances inside them, then scattering them as stardust when they die. The Earth and everything on it is made from this stardust.

The Universe today

Since the first stars and galaxies formed, the Universe has continued to grow and change. So what is the Universe like today and where does the Earth fit in?

> The planets are actually much more spread out than this. If the Sun was the size of an orange, then the Earth would be about 14 metres away, and Neptune would be over 400 metres (four football pitches) away!

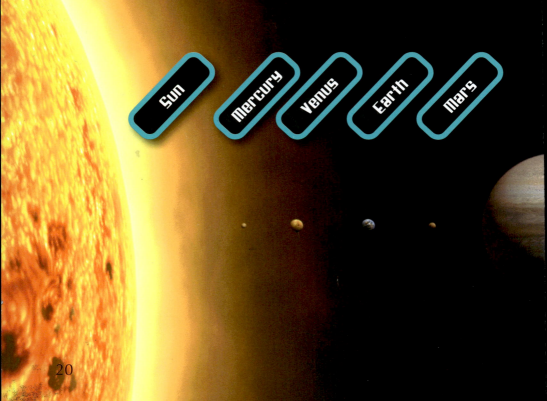

Eight planets

The Earth is a planet – a ball of rock 12,800 kilometres across. It orbits the Sun.

The Earth is one of eight planets orbiting the Sun. Mercury is nearest the Sun, followed by Venus, Earth, Mars, Jupiter, Saturn, Uranus and Neptune. The four nearest planets are smaller, and made of rock. The outer four planets are much bigger. They are made mostly of gas.

The Solar System

The planets are not the only things orbiting the Sun. Between Mars and Jupiter there is an area where millions of chunks of rock orbit the Sun. The rock pieces are called asteroids, and the area is the Asteroid Belt.
The biggest asteroid is nearly 1,000 kilometres across.

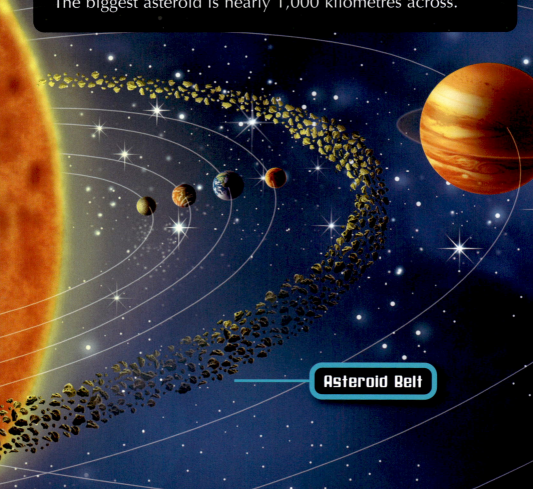

Asteroid Belt

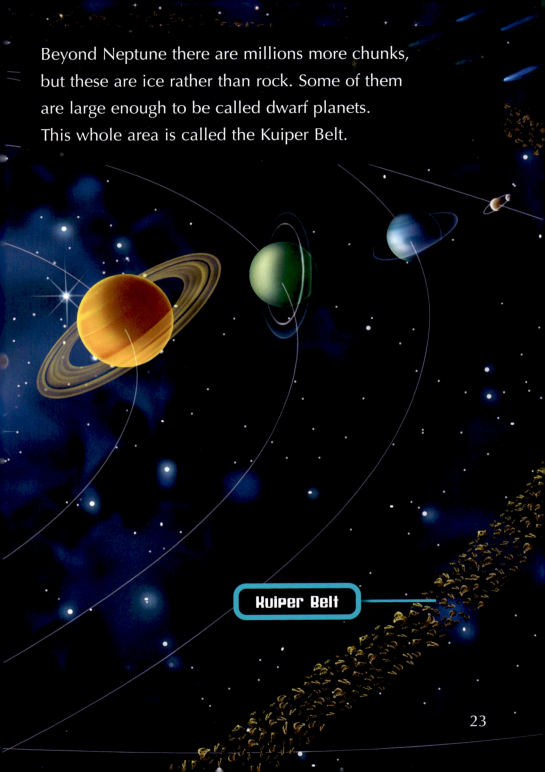

Beyond Neptune there are millions more chunks, but these are ice rather than rock. Some of them are large enough to be called dwarf planets. This whole area is called the Kuiper Belt.

Kuiper Belt

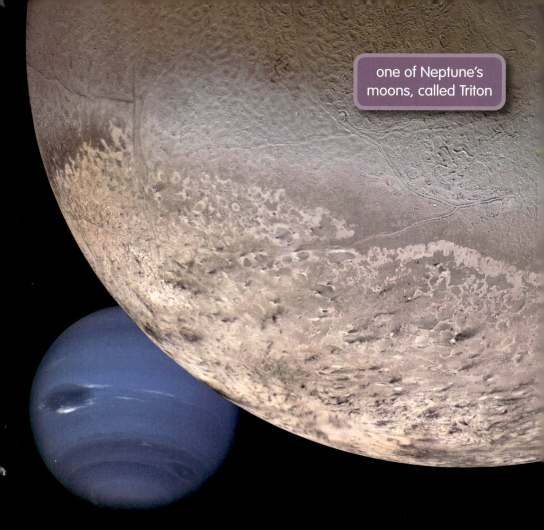

one of Neptune's moons, called Triton

Some planets have moons orbiting around them. The big gas planets have many moons – for instance, Jupiter has 63. Saturn, Uranus and Neptune also have rings. These are collections of small ice particles that form a ring around the planet.

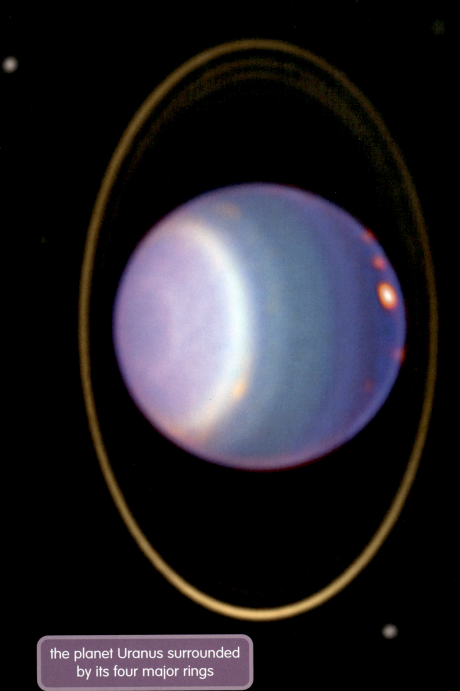

the planet Uranus surrounded by its four major rings

Even further out than these small ice particles, a huge cloud of comets orbits the Sun. Comets are small lumps of ice covered by a frozen crust of dust. Some comets travel far out into space but then briefly come close to the Sun. When this happens, the comet heats up. Some of the ice and dust boils off into space, making a long "tail".

Fact file

Some comets are **visible** from Earth during their time close to the Sun. The most famous is Halley's Comet, which appears every 76 years. It will next be visible in 2061.

This shows the Hale-Bopp comet over California, USA.

The Sun, planets and all the other chunks of rock and ice are together known as the Solar System. The whole system is held together by the pull of the Sun's gravity.

A spiral of stars

If you look at the sky on a dark, clear night, you'll see a faint "river" of white stretching across the sky. This is the Milky Way. If you look at it through a telescope, you'll see that it is made up of millions of faint stars. What you're seeing is the edge of our galaxy.

the Milky Way seen through a telescope from Earth

The Sun is one star in the Milky Way galaxy. The Milky Way is an enormous whirlpool of over 200 billion stars. From Earth, we cannot see the shape of the Milky Way because we are inside it, but scientists think it is a spiral galaxy with two arms.

This is how **astronomers** think the Milky Way looks when seen from above.

Groups and clusters

The Milky Way is not the only galaxy. There are billions of others. Not all are shaped like whirlpools. Some galaxies are round like footballs or oval like rugby balls. Some look like flying saucers.

other galaxy shapes

From studies of millions of galaxies, astronomers have created a map of the Universe. The map shows that galaxies are not spread out evenly. They form clumps and long strings, with large spaces between them.

Most galaxies are moving away from each other. But galaxies that are fairly close together are often attracted towards each other. Eventually they collide and form a bigger galaxy.

Fact file

One of the nearest galaxies to the Milky Way is another big spiral called Andromeda. It gets about four billion kilometres closer to the Milky Way each year. Even at this speed, Andromeda will not collide with the Milky Way for another four and a half billion years.

Discovering the Big Bang

We've known about the Big Bang for less than 100 years. So how did we learn about it? The story begins in the early 1900s. At the time, astronomers only knew about the Earth, the Solar System and the Milky Way galaxy. They knew nothing about the rest of the Universe.

At that time, astronomers were puzzled by small, fuzzy patches they saw among the stars. Some astronomers thought they were fairly close to Earth. Others thought they were much further away. The trouble was, there was no way of telling.

In 1912 an American astronomer called Henrietta Leavitt was studying special stars that seemed to flash: shining brightly then dimly, then brightly, then dimly. She found a way to work out the distance to these flashing stars by measuring their brightness and how fast they flashed. At last, astronomers had markers that could help them work out the distances to objects in space.

Henrietta Leavitt

Fact file

On a dark night, a small torch nearby can look as bright as a motorbike light 100 metres away. The motorbike light is much brighter, but it is further away, so less of its light reaches you. In the same way, a dim star that is quite close can look as bright as a brighter star that is further away.

Sirius looks like the brightest star in the night sky because it is the closest to Earth.

New galaxies

In 1917 a powerful new telescope was built at the Mount Wilson Observatory, near Los Angeles, in America. At the time, it was the biggest telescope in the world.

Another American, Edwin Hubble, used the new telescope to look at some of the fuzzy patches astronomers had been puzzling about for so long. In one patch, he found several flashing stars. When he took measurements of these stars, he discovered that they were incredibly far away. They were over 25 times further away than the furthest stars in the Milky Way. Hubble realised that the fuzzy patch was in fact another galaxy.

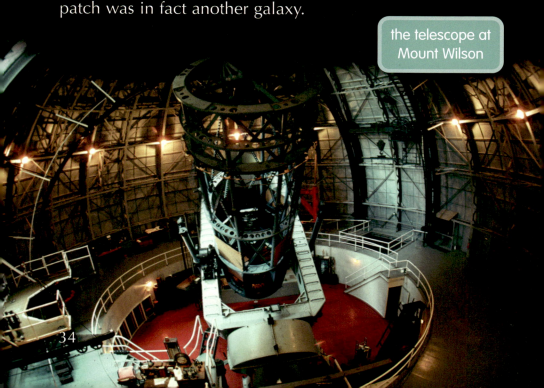

the telescope at Mount Wilson

Hubble began to search other fuzzy patches for flashing stars. He found that many of the patches were galaxies, even further from Earth than the first one.

With Hubble's discoveries, the Universe had grown from a single galaxy, the Milky Way, into a vast area containing millions of galaxies.

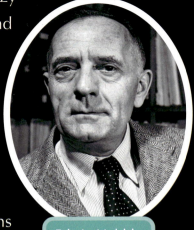

Edwin Hubble

This photo of distant galaxies was taken with a very powerful telescope.

The Big Bang theory

Until the 1920s, scientists thought that the Universe was unchanging. But when Hubble was studying distant galaxies, he made another discovery. He found that nearly every galaxy was moving away from the Earth. He realised that the whole Universe must be expanding!

This discovery was the beginning of the idea of the Big Bang, because if galaxies are moving away from each other today, then in the past they must have been closer together. If we go back far enough in time, we will reach a point when the whole Universe was packed into one tiny dot of space.

In 1927, a Belgian astronomer, Georges Lemaitre, was the first to suggest that the Universe began in a big bang. Most scientists thought the idea was crazy. Then, in the 1940s a Russian scientist called George Gamow took the Big Bang idea seriously, and worked out ways in which it could have happened. His ideas began to convince other scientists.

George Gamow

This huge telescope in Hawaii helps modern astronomers to see and measure the stars. The scientists who first came up with the idea of the Big Bang had to rely on much simpler and more basic equipment.

How do we know?

When it was first suggested, the Big Bang was only an idea. But since then, astronomers and other scientists have found lots of evidence that the Big Bang really happened.

Looking back in time

One of the main ways that astronomers have learnt about the Universe in the past, is by looking back in time.

How can we possibly look back in time? Well – we see things because of the light that comes from them. We can see the Sun, for instance, because light pours out from it.

Light travels incredibly fast. A light beam can travel seven and a half times around the world in one second. But because space is so big, light cannot cross the vast distances in an instant. Light from the Sun takes eight minutes to reach us on Earth.

Other stars are much further away than the Sun. Light coming from them takes years to reach us. So when we look at a distant object we are looking back in time, to when the light from that object set off on its journey to Earth.

Light from these stars takes about 440 years to reach Earth. The light we see started its journey when Queen Elizabeth I was queen of England.

39

Better telescopes

Astronomers today have much better telescopes than when Edwin Hubble was discovering distant galaxies. With bigger telescopes they can look out further into space, and so look back further in time.

In 1948, a telescope twice as big as Hubble's started work at the Palomar Observatory in San Diego, California. In the 1990s, two telescopes nearly four times as big as Hubble's were built in Hawaii. In 2009 an even bigger telescope began working in the Canary Islands.

Better as well as bigger

When we look at the stars from Earth, we are looking through a blanket of air over 100 kilometres thick. It's like looking out at the world through smudgy windows. Today's telescopes have found ways to use computers and lasers to almost get rid of this "smudginess".

This is the huge telescope which began working in the Canary Islands in 2009.

Telescopes in space

To get the best possible views of the Universe, a telescope needs to be in space.

Over the past 50 years, scientists have sent many instruments up into space to study the stars.
The best known is the Hubble Space Telescope (HST). This was launched in 1990 and is still working. It has produced some of the clearest and most spectacular views of the Universe yet.

the Hubble Space Telescope

This photograph was taken with the Hubble Space Telescope and shows newly formed stars.

Seeing in different ways

Another way to learn more about the Universe is to use telescopes that see in a different way from us. There are all kinds of light that are invisible to our eyes, including radio waves and X-rays. Some telescopes are designed to pick up these invisible rays.

Radio waves

Radio waves are used to send radio and TV programmes all over the world. But there are also radio waves coming from space. Some telescopes are designed to pick up these radio waves. Radio telescopes can see the tiny ball of rock left after a large star has exploded. This gives out no light, but produces strong radio signals.

Infra-red and X-rays

Two other kinds of telescope look at infra-red light and X-rays. Infra-red telescopes sense heat. They can see through dark dust clouds to the stars inside them.

X-ray telescopes pick up high-energy events. If a galaxy is producing X-rays, it means that it is giving off huge amounts of energy.

The Crab Nebula is the remains of a huge star explosion that happened nearly 1,000 years ago. This picture of the Crab Nebula was taken using X-rays.

Fact file

There are scientific projects that search for aliens using radio telescopes. The scientists are looking for radio signals that could have been sent out by alien life forms.

45

Future discoveries

In the last 100 years astronomers have learnt a huge amount about the Universe and its history. But as they learn more there are new questions to answer, new things to discover. Astronomers are already planning new experiments and building new telescopes to find out more.

A new telescope

In 2014, a new telescope will be launched into space. It is called the James Webb Space Telescope (JWST). The new telescope is over twice as big as the Hubble Space Telescope. It will be positioned a million miles from Earth, four times further away than the Moon.

The JWST is designed to **detect** infra-red waves rather than light. It will be able to look further and see more than any telescope we have today.

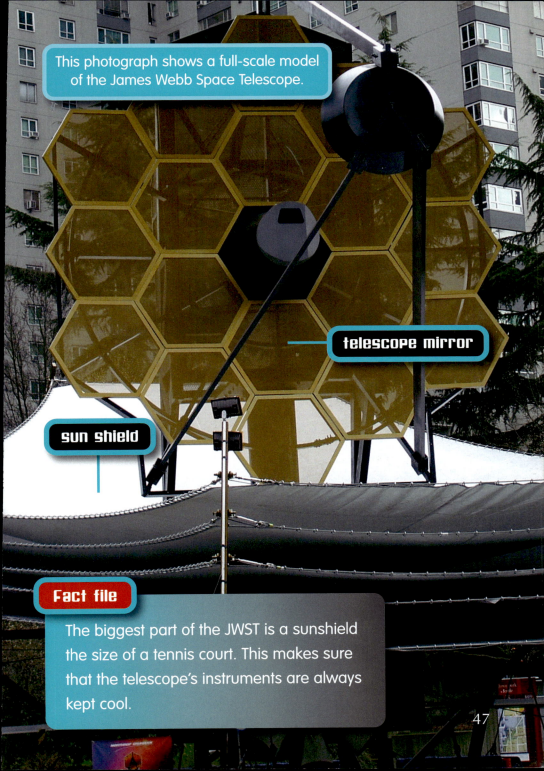

This photograph shows a full-scale model of the James Webb Space Telescope.

telescope mirror

sun shield

Fact file

The biggest part of the JWST is a sunshield the size of a tennis court. This makes sure that the telescope's instruments are always kept cool.

The future Universe

So what about the future? Does what we know about the past help us predict what will happen next?

We know from Hubble's work that the Universe is expanding. There are three main possibilities for what might happen next. The Universe could continue to expand at the same speed, for ever and ever.

three ways that the Universe could change in the future

1. The Universe keeps expanding at the same rate.

2. The Universe expands faster and faster.

3. The Universe expands and then contracts again.

A second possibility is that the Universe will expand faster and faster as time goes on. In both these cases, the Universe will go on forever.

The third option is that the expansion of the Universe is slowing down. If this is true, then at some point it will stop expanding altogether, and begin to **contract**. It will get smaller and smaller, and eventually end in a "big crunch".

Most of the evidence suggests that the Universe will not shrink again: it will go on expanding and expanding.

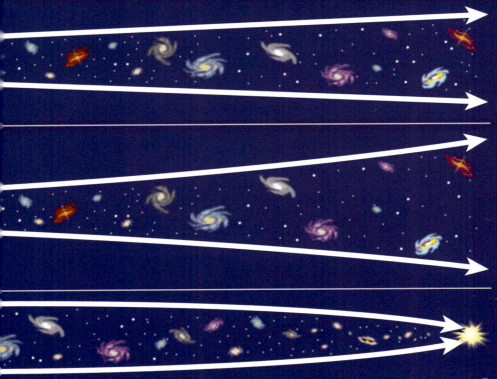

"big crunch"

Some answers and new questions

Since astronomers first came up with the idea of
the Big Bang, they have learnt so much more about
the Universe. But there is still much more to find out.
Was there anything *before* the Big Bang? Can we learn
more about the first stars? How much further can we see
into the past?

The new instruments being built today should give us
more information. But **astronomy** changes fast.
As scientists build new instruments, they make
new discoveries. And with new discoveries, there are
new questions to answer, and new scientists are needed
to answer them. Perhaps you could be one of them?

This photograph shows two galaxies colliding before they form one large galaxy.

51

Glossary

astronomers	scientists who study stars, planets and other objects in space
astronomy	the study of stars, planets and other objects in space
billion	a thousand million; it can be written as "1,000,000,000"
contract	shrink
detect	find
nuclear explosion	a very big explosion caused by the energy that's released when tiny particles called "atoms" are split open
orbit	the path a moon or planet takes as it goes round another planet or a star
substance	anything that has mass (weight) and occupies space
theory	idea
transparent	see-through
trillion	a thousand billion; it can be written as "1,000,000,000,000"
visible	able to be seen

Index

Asteroid Belt 22

astronomers 29, 30, 32, 34, 36, 37, 38, 40, 46, 50

comets 26, 27

Earth 2, 4, 14, 19, 20, 21, 24, 26, 28, 29, 32, 33, 35, 36, 38, 39, 40, 46

elements 18, 19

energy 4, 6, 7, 10, 44

explosion 2, 3, 4, 19, 45

galaxies 14, 16, 20, 28, 29, 30, 31, 32, 34, 35, 36, 40, 44

Gamow, George 36

gas 6, 8, 9, 12, 13, 14, 15, 16, 21, 24

gravity 14, 16, 27

helium 18

Hubble, Edwin 34, 35, 36, 40, 48

Hubble Space Telescope 42, 46

hydrogen 4, 12, 13, 16, 18

infra-red 44, 46

James Webb Space Telescope 46, 47

Kuiper Belt 23

Leavitt, Henrietta 32

Lemaitre, Georges 36

light 6, 7, 10, 11, 12, 33, 38, 39, 44, 46

liquid 6, 8, 9, 14

matter 8, 9, 10

Milky Way 28, 29, 30, 31, 32, 34, 35

moon 14, 24, 46

particles 9, 10, 12, 24, 26

planets 14, 20, 21, 22, 23, 24, 27

radio waves 44

Solar System 22, 27, 32

solid 6, 8, 14

stardust 18, 19

stars 12, 14, 15, 16, 17, 18, 19, 20, 28, 29, 32, 33, 34, 35, 38, 39, 40, 42, 44, 45, 50

Sun 2, 6, 10, 12, 14, 16, 17, 20, 21, 22, 26, 27, 29, 38

supernova 19

telescope 28, 34, 35, 40, 41, 42, 44, 45, 46, 47

X-rays 44, 45

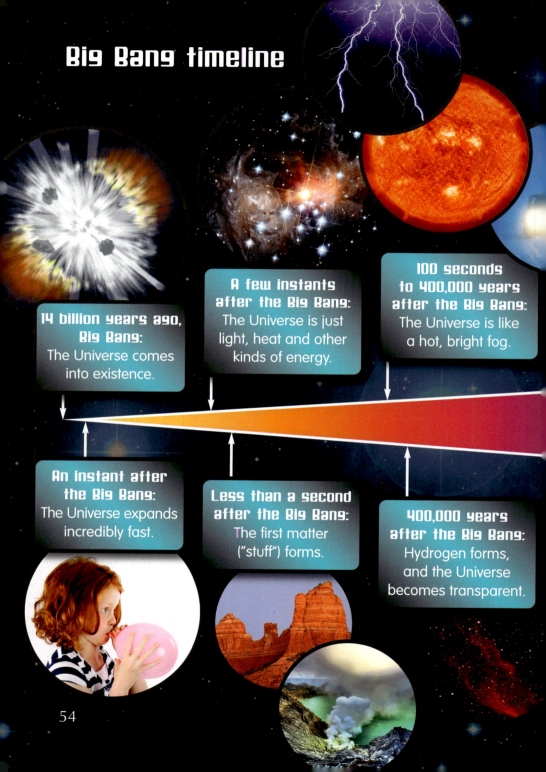

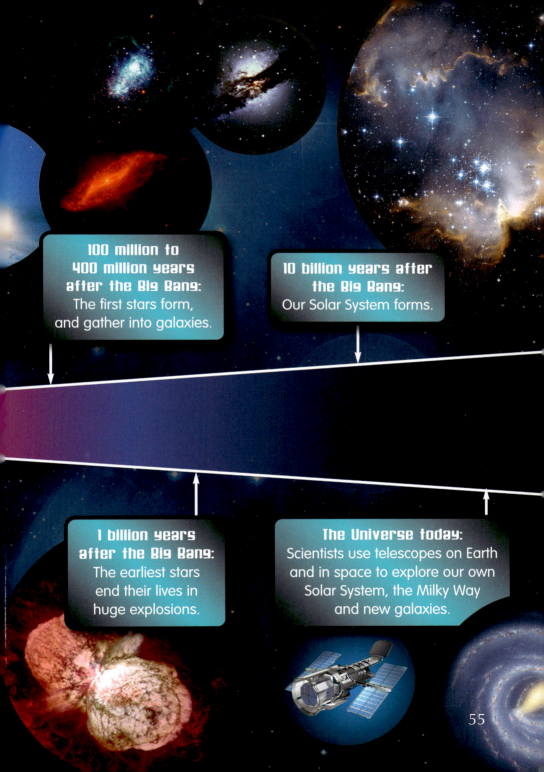

100 million to 400 million years after the Big Bang: The first stars form, and gather into galaxies.

10 billion years after the Big Bang: Our Solar System forms.

1 billion years after the Big Bang: The earliest stars end their lives in huge explosions.

The Universe today: Scientists use telescopes on Earth and in space to explore our own Solar System, the Milky Way and new galaxies.

Ideas for reading

Written by Linda Pagett B.Ed (hons), M.Ed
Lecturer and Educational Consultant

Learning objectives: use knowledge of different organisation features of texts; use and explore different question types; present a spoken argument sequencing points logically

Curriculum links: Science: Earth, Sun and Moon

Interest words: astronomy, asteroid, billion, comet, hydrogen, helium, gravity, Kuiper Belt, Milky Way, nuclear explosion, particle, star islands, substance, supernova, solar, spiral, Sirius, telescope, theory, transparent

Resources: writing materials, ICT, spheres of various sizes including beach ball, pea and small bead

Getting started

This book can be read over two or more guided reading sessions.

- Ask a child to read aloud the blurb and discuss the first two questions it raises. Find out what the children already know about the early Universe, e.g. *How do you think the Universe began? What do you think it was like before the Universe began?*
- Ask children to make notes in three columns with the headings: "What we know"; "What we want to know"; "What we found out", completing the first two columns before they start to read the book.
- Scan the pages of the book together highlighting the features of non-fiction books, e.g. fact files, captions, glossary, index, etc.
- Turn to the glossary and make sure the children understand the terms used.

Reading and responding

- Working in pairs, ask the children to read several consecutive chapters, using the contents page as a guide. Make sure that all the sections are read.
- Ask children to make notes while they read, summarising the main points.